A New
Dawn

Dawn Miller

A New
Dawn

More than a new day, a journey
from broken to beautiful

TATE PUBLISHING
AND ENTERPRISES, LLC

Published by Tate Publishing & Enterprises, LLC
127 E. Trade Center Terrace | Mustang, Oklahoma 73064 USA
1.888.361.9473 | www.tatepublishing.com

Tate Publishing is committed to excellence in the publishing industry. The company reflects the philosophy established by the founders, based on Psalm 68:11,
"The Lord gave the word and great was the company of those who published it."

Book design copyright © 2016 by Tate Publishing, LLC. All rights reserved.
Cover design by Norlan Balazo
Interior design by Richell Balansag

Published in the United States of America

ISBN: 978-1-68207-086-4
Biography & Autobiography / Religious
15.11.03

ACKNOWLEDGMENTS

What an honor it is to have the opportunity to share this project. However, I could not have done so on my own. I am truly thankful for the support and encouragement I have received from so many wonderful people, all of which I am not able to mention individually, but you and I both know who you are.

First and foremost, I give God thanks and all the glory for the privilege to share His story of my life. I pray that you see Him throughout the pages of this book.

I also want to thank the three most important men in my life, my husband and two sons, for their enduring love and support. Chris, as my granny always said, "You could have searched the whole world over and never found someone as good as Chris." Thank you for loving me as Christ loves His bride. Kajun and Rylan, you mean the world to me, and I am truly blessed to be the mother of two of the most amazing young men I know.

And a great BIG thank you to my mother. Mom, you have been constant throughout my journey. Thank you for teaching me by example the two most important principles of life: loving God first and loving others. You are my hero!

Lastly, I can't go without thanking a few of my darling friends who have helped so much with the practical details of writing this book. Charity Mouck and Kathy Lay, thank you for your willingness to read and re-read this project. Thank you for sharing your expertise and instruction, for which I am enriched. Mostly, thank you for your constant support. And a quick shout-out to a more recent special friend and kindred spirit, Jamie Rasor. Thank you for listening to God and giving me the nudge to try again.

CONTENTS

FOREWORD

The Bible states in Psalm 51:5 "Behold, I was shapen in iniquity; and in sin did my mother conceive me."

This is a literal scripture for me as my conception was a result of sin. A mistake, a big oops, a "you got busted" are all descriptions of my literal beginnings. What a way to define one's start of life. And if not for the grace of God, I would have allowed that to define me instead of the truth of who I was and who I am.

See, it is so very easy for us to view ourselves in and by things that have happened to us, things that are said about us, how we think others perceive us, and not by the truth of who we were created to be. God said we were created in His image. Therefore, He defines who we are by divine design. Furthermore, He defines our worth and value by the cross of Christ. Anything else is false identity and misappropriated value.

You are who God says you are.

1

Against All Odds

Being seventeen, a senior in high school, and expecting was not accepted well in the early seventies. However, that was my mother. Even though they tried to tell her she couldn't continue in school and graduate, she was determined to do so and with her class. She was not the only one who had such determination. Her mom, my granny, was just as determined that she graduate and do so with her class. Granny was one whom you really didn't want to cross. She was small in stature but mighty in terms of a strong will and reminded me of Granny in the *Beverly Hillbillies*. Granny made sure that the powers that be at the school understood that her daughter would, in fact, graduate with her class. It has been told to me that Granny readily pointed out that if there were any problems with it, she would be sure to let the local reporters know of the young girls who had been in the same condition but had abortions. As stated earlier, you really didn't want to mess with my granny.

Since my mom was due to deliver the end of October, it was concluded that she would not attend the fall semester but would return to school in the spring and graduate with her class. Now that the school issues were resolved, it was time to work on my pappy. It just wasn't accepted and was considered a bad reflection on the family for a young girl to become pregnant out of wedlock. My mother was just seventeen and had plenty of "growing up" to do. Pappy, her father, decided that she would have to give me up for adoption. One of my mom's sisters suggested that my mom just have an abortion. That would be the best way to save the family from being a spectacle for others to ridicule for her misbehavior. Thankfully for me, neither of these happened. Again, Granny managed to work that out as well as she told my mom that she would help her take care of me.

However, with all the shame and embarrassment my mom felt, she tried to end the pregnancy by inducing a miscarriage. Her first attempt was to jump off the porch roof of the house in hopes that this would work. No such luck! She then tried another sure potion to get the job done. She drank something they called mistletoe tea. Yet again, her attempt failed. After coming to grips with the fact that this was just going to be, she went on with life as best she could.

In the meantime, my father, who was stationed at the Grissom Air Force Base in Bunker Hill, Indiana, went AWOL when my mom told him she was going to have a baby. This situation could cause him some pretty serious issues. That didn't last long as they caught him and put him in military jail. There the arrangements began for my mom and father to marry. Being that my father's dad was a minister and pastor, it was considered the right thing for all involved.

Plans changed. With the counsel of my grandparents' pastor, Mom decided not to marry my father. The consideration was that if he had left her once, he just might do so again. Therefore, they did not marry. Each went their separate ways, and life went on for the both of them. They were young and still had things they wanted to do. After all, neither of them had planned for the pregnancy in the first place.

2

It's a Girl

October came and went, and Mom was still awaiting my arrival. Finally, on November 2 at 3:55 a.m., I arrived. Now it all became a reality. Mom's new life, with that of a child to raise, began. Seventeen with a little baby girl who was totally dependent on her—what a great responsibility. Still, at home, she assumed her responsibility with the help of her mom and dad.

Time seemed to go by so fast, and it was already the second semester of the academic year. Mom had to double her classes so she could graduate in May with the rest of her class. She also took a job at a nursing home, working second shift to help support me. Granny would watch me while Mom was at school and working. Granny would have me sleep during the afternoon and evening so that when my mom got off work at 11:00 p.m., she could spend some time with me before going to bed. This was the routine she managed through the semester. I'm sure this was quite the challenge, but my mom was determined to make it work, and that she did.

I am told that one day while my mom was at work, my father stopped by in an attempt to see me for the first time. Once again, Granny intervened. She was not interested in my father having anything to do with me due to his absence up to this point. She proceeded to meet him at the door with what my father said was a shotgun. Now I'm not sure Granny was even big enough to hold a shotgun, but nevertheless, my father didn't stay around to clarify. From that day on, he never tried to see me again.

3

A Father for Me

Time marched on, and Mom was doing fine as a single mom. However, she started receiving some backlash from one of her older brothers about living at home and having her parents support her. That was not her intention, but it wasn't easy to make it on your own and support a little one. She was determined to give it a shot, though. Mom moved to Anderson, Indiana, upon taking a job at a van conversion shop. It was there she met a gentleman. They started dating, and not too long afterward, Mom decided to marry her newfound friend, Mr. Larry. He was fifteen years older than Mom, and it seemed that he could offer a stable life for her and her daughter.

In just a short time, Mom became pregnant again. She was not ready to have another baby and quickly came to the realization that marrying for convenience doesn't really work out so well. After about four months of being married, she decided to file for divorce. With that decision and the news of being pregnant came the questions of what to do about the baby. She knew she could not support two little ones on her own. So with an overwhelming sense of inadequacy, Mom decided to have an abortion. She has explained that as soon as the procedure was taking place, she heard a baby cry. To this day, she says she is still haunted by it and her only means of coping is the knowledge that God has forgiven her for that decision.

At twenty years of age, Mom married again but this time for love. She married a friend of hers, Glen, whom she had attended church with since she was about twelve years old. He was just shy of three years younger than her, but that didn't matter, especially to him, as he'd had a crush on her for some time. Even when she was pregnant with me, his feelings for her didn't change. In fact, on the day I was born, he rode his bicycle about fifteen miles one way just to see me. He was a consistent visitor even after my arrival. He stayed the course while Mom was dating and even when she married Mr. Larry. One day, he asked to see me, so my mom took me to my granny's house, and I'm told that when he walked through the door, my eyes lit up and I started saying, "Daddy, Daddy!"

When Mom had accepted the marriage proposal from Mr. Larry, Glen decided to join the US Army. He told my mom that if she changed her mind, he would come back after basic training and he would wait for her. Mom had married in December, and Glen left for basic training in January of 1977. Upon his return the following July, Mom—now divorced—was available and accepting of his proposal to marry him. I was two and a half years old and the flower girl at their wedding. Now with a mommy and daddy, our life as a family was off to a great start.

4

---◦ᲔᲔᲕ◦---

On the Move

Joining the army was an effort for Daddy to start a career in hopes to support his "already made" family. No complaints, though, because he was in love with my mom and we came as a package deal. Not long after his return from basic training, he was stationed in Fort Polk, Louisiana. So we had to pack up and head off to a whole new world, at least to us. We moved to a small town named Anacoco. It was about twenty miles from the Fort Polk army base.

Wow, what a scary start: hundreds of miles away from home, two people who were practically teenagers starting a life of their own with a little girl to raise—nevertheless, that was exactly what they did. Although he was still just a young man, Daddy assumed his responsibility to support his family. Mom continued with her consuming responsibility of caring for me. She would have told you then, and even now, that I was and still am her pride and joy. The very thing that mom was ashamed of and which society looked down on became the very reason of her existence. It's amazing how something so tiny can have such a huge impact, a life-changing one. And with that, she knew that she needed to find a church to get involved in as she was raised in church herself. Even though she had not been committed over the years, she felt God pulling at her heartstrings for a very long time.

So without too much delay, she found a church in the little town we lived in, and she took me for the first time on a Sunday evening. Even though Daddy had been brought up in church most of his life as well, he wasn't quite ready to commit. Mom still continued to go, and about a month later and with lots of tears from my mom, Daddy started to attend with us. From then on, we attended and became heavily involved in the church.

Mom became a Sunday school teacher. I must say, she was the best Sunday school teacher I ever had. Daddy played the guitar for the praise team. We were over the bus ministry and would pick up kids for Sunday school. Later, my mom and daddy became the youth leaders and continued to do so for several years. So my heritage is one of great involvement and commitment to God and the church.

Just over a year after our arrival in Louisiana, we had a new addition to our family. Mom delivered me a little brother. He was named after his father, Glen, but we called him Buddy. The arrival of my little brother meant more responsibility and necessities. Money was tight, as the only income we had was from Daddy working at the base. Daddy oftentimes had to hitchhike to work, which was about twenty miles from where we lived. However, with a growing family, he did what was necessary to provide for the four of us.

A couple of years after my brother was born, Daddy was honorably discharged from the US Army. He then had to find other forms of employment to support us. Since they wanted to be close to their families, Daddy and Mom decided to move back to Indiana. We stayed with my mom's parents, and Daddy began to look for a job. Due to historically high unemployment rates and a mild recession in the early eighties, he was unable to find a job. After three months of trying, we moved back to Louisiana, and Daddy started working construction at Fort Polk, where he had previously been stationed. Once again, we settled in, and Louisiana became our home.

5

The Beginning of a Long Journey

Sometime around four years of age, things started to happen—or malfunction, you might say. My first memory of the beginning of a long journey ahead was of Daddy giving me a bath. This didn't seem strange as most people would think that it is pretty natural for a father to give his daughter a bath. However, I did not know that I was born out of wedlock and that the man whom my mom was married to was not my father. "Stop, Daddy, that hurts," I remember saying. Those words still ring loud and clear in the crevices of my memory. I tried to tell my mom that Daddy washed me too hard; however, it wasn't easy for a child to explain the start of molestation, let alone understand it. So bath after bath from my daddy was marred by the hard washing and drying. As I grew older and began to bathe myself, the inappropriate touching and behavior from Daddy just carried on outside of bath time.

I remember coming home from first grade one day, and Daddy was sitting in the pink—nowadays, one might call it mauve—chair in my bedroom. He told me to come to him and he would help me change my clothes. Again, this wasn't anything unnatural as many fathers help change their kids' clothes. But somehow, changing my clothes involved a whole lot more than that. I can even remember what I was wearing at the time. I had on a cream velvet shirt and a little skirt.

Somewhere in the process of being changed by my daddy, I ended up straddling him, with my legs across the arms of the chair. He must have been changing his clothes as well because he became exposed and started to rub my private area with his. See, all these things would make me Daddy's little girl. Or at least that was what was being relayed to me. And isn't that what every little girl dreams of being? It just didn't seem to make sense to me, even in my little innocent mind. Although I didn't quite understand what was going on, I still felt ashamed but didn't know what to do. So it continued day after day, week after week, month after month, and year after year.

One might ask the question, "Why didn't you just tell your mom?" And that seems to be such a simple and applicable solution. However, most times it doesn't quite work that way when you are in the situation. Thoughts of how she would respond paralyzed any thought of telling. Trust and believe me, I was definitely told enough not to tell or negative things would happen. If I told her, she would not love me anymore. It was my fault, anyway. Others would look down on our family if they knew. I surely wouldn't be Daddy's little girl anymore. These were just a few of the thoughts I can remember running through my mind.

As time went on, different things continued to happen. I remember when I was about six or seven years old playing what Daddy referred to as a game where I had to hold his privates and go back and forth, counting to see how long he could go before releasing. Over and over again, game after game, this continued. Even though I really didn't understand the depth of what was going on, something inside of me knew that this wasn't right. I felt dirty. My innocence was being tainted. Therefore, this led to skewing my developing views on such subjects. I questioned, *Did all little girls do this with their daddy?* It just didn't feel right.

Since Daddy worked nights and was home during the day while my mom worked, I was often made to lie down with him. It didn't take very long for me to become unclothed and lying on his chest as he groped and fondled places that should not have been touched. *Why was this happening?* I often asked myself. *Does this really make me Daddy's little girl?* It seemed that other little girls were happy to be with their daddies, and I wasn't feeling that.

It was around the age of eight that I was introduced to oral sex. The first time it happened to me, my body responded in the natural, pleasurable way of which I had no control.

However, it made me feel as though I was very bad because I shouldn't feel such by something that I knew was wrong. I hated what was happening, but my body was responding differently. The guilt and shame was overwhelming. I hated it and started hating Daddy for what he was doing. It was especially difficult for me when he would be harsh to my mom about something because I knew what he was doing. And I thought he didn't deserve to have her do so much for him.

When I was still around the age of eight, Daddy decided to come clean and told my mom a little bit of what had been taking place. I do not believe that the exhaustive truth was shared, but nevertheless, he alluded to the fact that he had made some poor choices. He told her he was sorry and that it would never happen again. I was later asked by my mom as to why I didn't tell her. I shared with her my fear that she would be mad at me and not love me anymore. She assured me that this would never be the case.

So on with life of a brand-new start, or at least that was my thought. Yes, you guessed it. Just a few days later, and we were back at it again. Now you may question, How does this happen? I'm not sure I can give a definitive answer. I do believe Daddy was sorry; however, he had some serious issues that were not being taken care of as they should have. He had some ghosts in his closet that he had never dealt with. Daddy watched his father molest his sisters during his childhood. This does not by any means validate or excuse his personal choices, but it does enlighten to the probability of why.

There are a few more memories forever etched in my head, one of which I think I came the closest to dying from fear. It was time for bed, and I remember being frightened for some reason and asked my mom if I could sleep on the floor in her bedroom. She consented and made me a pallet on the floor at the foot of her bed. Daddy was already in bed and asleep, or so it appeared. After Mom was in bed for a little bit, Daddy got up out of bed and quietly came down and kneeled at the foot of the pallet where I was lying. He began to try and fondle me.

You can imagine the fear that gripped my heart. I knew if Mom woke up all hell would break loose. Well, that was exactly what happened. Words cannot describe the fear that overtook me in that moment when I heard her voice as she sat up, yelling at Daddy. I literally felt like I was going to die. My heart started racing, and it seemed as though I could not catch my breath. Mom got out of bed and started looking for the gun she had hidden in her closet. She wasn't able to find it, and if she had, that would have been the end of the story more than likely.

I knew that the pistol was on top of the fridge. I knew if she found it someone would most likely die that night. My heart felt like it was going to literally pound out of my chest. I could hear the rage in her voice. She was overcome by it.

Daddy went on to the bathroom, and Mom followed him. I could hear them arguing as I sat there quietly praying.

See, Mom had gone to bed without any acknowledgment from Daddy. No kiss good night or even the words themselves were shared. Yet he got up out of bed and came down to the floor where I laid. He tried to convince Mom that he was just telling me good night and I wasn't about to say anything differently. The poor excuse was not acceptable to Mom with the backdrop of Daddy's lack of responsiveness when she went to bed. Needless to say, she was beyond livid. The rage she felt inside warned her that she could do some things she may later regret. Finally, with no definitive response and with a lack of emotion from Daddy, everyone went back to bed. Mom and I slept in my twin bed in my room the remainder of the night. We all managed to survive the night. However, it was not enough to stop the continued abuse.

In the meantime, as all these things were going on, my brother became very sick. It all started after a fall during church camp, where he was tripped and he hit his head on the concrete slab. After that, he just seemed to keep having problems with headaches.

Speaking of camp, those five weeks of the summer were the most normal weeks of our lives. Our family stayed on the grounds in a cabin and later in our own RV as we worked the concession stand. I made cotton candy and had a blast at it. Those days were some of my fondest memories as a kid. The reality of home seemed to disappear momentarily.

Back to my brother, Buddy. Things began to worsen, and his headaches became so severe that I would have to sit and rub his forehead to give him some relief. He then started to become delusional. Mom finally took him to the doctor, and they diagnosed him with strep throat. They treated him, but he didn't get any better. Back at the doctor again, they increased his antibiotic dosage to that of an adult's. Still, he didn't seem to be improving. He continued to have severe headaches. Mom decided to take him for a second opinion as it seemed we were getting nowhere with the current doctor.

Mom took him to a pediatric doctor in DeRidder, Louisiana, about thirty miles away from home. The facility and doctors there were more reputable than those in our town. Upon arrival, the doctors decided to perform a spinal tap on Buddy to see what may be the issue. Before doing so, Dr. Griffin, the pediatrician, decided to take a quick evaluation of Buddy. When he looked into his eyes, he was alarmed as he noted swelling of the brain. This was serious. The spinal tap was immediately canceled because if it were performed with swelling on the brain, it would have been fatal. Buddy was then rushed to Christus St. Frances Cabrini Hospital in Alexandria, Louisiana. It was about an hour away. He was to have emergency brain surgery. They thought he had a brain tumor, but it turned out that he had an aneurysm that clotted in the right lobe of his brain. They had to go in and remove a portion of his brain. Amazingly, it was a portion of the brain that we do not use. This was a miracle. God continued to perform several more miracles during the time of Buddy's progress and recovery.

It took several months to get his medications regulated. And the doctors had told my mom that he would be on some of the meds for the rest of his life, especially the one to control seizures. But God said differently. Buddy doesn't take any of those meds now and is in his midthirties. That's not all. You can only imagine how costly such a procedure and medical care was. Even with no insurance coverage—as Daddy was laid off—we were still responsible for close to fifty thousand dollars in medical bills. My mom began payment on this in increments of five dollars a month as that was all we could afford. Later, we received a letter stating that our portion of the medical expense had been written off. Yet another miracle!

I was later informed that before this incident with my brother, Daddy was planning to adopt me. With the turn of events with Buddy, this became impossible. In fact, every time the funds were available and adoption was to transpire, something would happen with my brother that would require the use of the allotted funds, making the adoption impossible. Looking back now, I know that God was working behind the scenes. He was working for a greater plan.

6

The Secret Is Out

When I was in the sixth grade, my peers began to call me a bastard. I wasn't sure what it even meant but knew it wasn't nice. So I started to inquire to my mom as to why my friends were calling me such a name. Apparently, my mom had shared her story with some of her close friends, who discussed the details in the company of their kids, hence making it back to me. At that time, I was clueless to the story. My mom and stepdad had planned not to tell me until I turned eighteen. In the meantime, the plan was for my stepdad to adopt me. With thoughtful consideration of what to do, my mom decided that she should share the details with me now instead of waiting and me getting bits and pieces of information from others. So finally, at eleven years old, I got the rest of the story.

Mom proceeded to tell me that my stepdad was not my father. She handed me a letter that she received from my biological father's parents in return to one she had written them when I was eight. Knowing that my father's parents were pastors of a church in Marshall, Illinois, she thought she would write to them and let them know that she was raising me in the church and I had given my life to Christ at eight years of age at a youth camp.

The response to my mom's letter was basically the expression of their approval and gratefulness of her raising me in the church. However, it stated that my father had a family, and they weren't sure if he had shared his past with them, so they thought it best to leave things the way they were.

That reality was a little difficult to take. At eleven, I interpreted it as them saying that they really didn't want to be bothered with me. That was a little much for me, a young girl, to process, let alone try to understand why my mom had kept this information from me. Especially since I was trying to make sense of all the things my stepdad was doing to me. Truth is, it simply didn't make any sense at all. I felt betrayed, unloved, and unwanted.

7

Who's Your Daddy?

I began to resent my stepdad for what he was doing to me. I resented my mom for keeping the truth from me. The wonder of what my father was like momentarily offset the resentment of him not trying to be involved in my life. I remember looking for him when we were out and about, just hoping to run into him. I remember men having their names engraved on their belts, and I would look to see if maybe—just maybe—I'd find him, John, that way. There were so many questions I had that only he could answer. And apparently, they would remain unanswered as it was made clear that he had his own life to live.

Nevertheless, I held on to the letter and the curiosity of knowing my father and his family. I started to pray about meeting my father someday. There seemed to be a huge empty space in knowing that an important part of me was missing. It was during that time that the Scripture in Psalm 34:18 (NLT) became real to me. It says, "The LORD is close to the brokenhearted; he rescues those whose spirits are crushed." I felt Him near, as I would cry out to Him often. God became my DADDY!, just as the latter portion of Romans 8:15 (NLT) says: "Instead, you received God's Spirit when he adopted you as his own children. Now we call him, 'Abba, Father.'" That means that God adopted me and He became my DADDY!

As I continued through my journey, this awesome truth became my rock. The older I got, the more I understood, and to this day, I still call Him DADDY. It is very literal for me.

8

•⚬ᎶᎩᎾ⚬•

The Journey Continues

Things weren't getting any better at home as far as the abuse was concerned. The older I got, the more resentful I became. I remember a very close call one evening as my stepdad called me to his room. He had some Vaseline and told me to lie down on the bed. I was old enough and exposed to enough by then to know what that meant. He had every intention of trying to go all the way. I don't mean to be crude here, but I knew that with his adult manhood if the inevitable happened, it would cause some serious damage to me as I was a little girl. As he began to apply the Vaseline, I began to pray out loud. It wasn't too long before the commotion alarmed my brother and he began to beat on the door. Finally, my stepdad looked at me and asked, "What did you think I was going to do?" He then replied that he wasn't going to do anything. Well, frankly, he'd already done too much, period. I knew what his intentions were that evening, but I truly believe that my DADDY answered a little girl's prayer that day.

I know that this promotes many unanswered questions for those who have suffered from any type of abuse or misfortune. Why? If He is God, then why doesn't He stop this? I asked those same questions many times myself. But I must say that it is not because He can't. However, I have come to the conclusion that we were all given the freedom of choice, and unfortunately, when we make bad choices, there are consequences to be suffered and most of the time not only for the one who makes the choice but also for anyone who is affected by such choice.

As I grew older, I was able to avoid a number of contact episodes. However, the invasion of privacy became a constant. I would often catch my stepdad peeping through the cracks of my door as I was dressing. He would stand outside my window at times, trying to catch a glimpse of me changing clothes. There were times that my brother, mostly when I was younger, would throw one of his little stuffed animals through a glassless window between the laundry room/bedroom and bathroom to alarm me that my stepdad, his father, was watching me as I bathed.

I remember when I was younger and my little girlfriends would come over, I would be sure to sit in front of them while we took a bath in an effort to hide them from the Peeping Tom. So in my early teen years, this became super frustrating as I felt as if I was always trying to hide while bathing or changing clothes when he was around. My resentment seemed to escalate the older I got because I understood that all the invasion of my body and privacy was not normal, and I wanted it to stop.

I was getting to the point where I could not keep pretending that we had the perfect little family. I couldn't hold it in anymore. I felt like I was going to go crazy on one hand, but on the other hand, felt like I would be an utter disappointment to all who respected us for what they thought we were. After all, we were heavily involved in our local church and my stepdad was the youth leader. Surely that meant we were a functional family. However, I have learned that the functionality of a family does not come from titles, monetary values, or positions. Those things can be very misleading.

It was a struggle for me in my early teen years to process through the fact that my stepdad would get up and speak to the congregation and they would respond and all the while I knew what he was really like at home. This didn't make much sense to me then. Now, looking back, I understand some things about my DADDY that I hadn't yet discovered as a child and teenager. See, He is faithful to His Word regardless of the messenger and honors the sincerity of one's heart when responding to His Word.

9

---•ᏀᎹᏂ•---

Enough

So at the point of *enough*, I decided to talk to someone. It was the summer before I turned sixteen, and we were on our way to church camp with my mom's best friend. For some reason, my mom wasn't with us. It was my brother and I. As we were making the hour drive to the campgrounds, I began to share bits and pieces—without specific details— of what was going on and the fact that I just couldn't keep pretending anymore. For my mom's best friend, it was quite a bit to process. And then "What to do?" was the question. Without any immediate answers, we started our week at camp.

Fear of what the future held for us and our family, with the thought of the truth being brought to light, was a bit overwhelming for my brother. He didn't eat much that week as the situation was nagging at him. Our parents were to come to the campgrounds at the end of the week, then what? That was where it all began to come to an end.

Upon their arrival, my mom noted right away that my brother had lost weight. The questions began. Not too long after they arrived, both my mom and my stepdad were called into the office of the concession stand. It just so happened that the manager of the concession stand was our pastor as well. Things started to become unveiled. Much to my mom's dismay, she found out that the abuse had not stopped. Much to our pastor's dismay, he found out it entailed much more than he had ever imagined. Needless to say, both were crushed by the truth.

Now it became my turn to talk. I just told my mom that I couldn't do it anymore. I told her that it had to be me or him. Needless to say, without hesitation, she declared it was me. The next few weeks and months seemed like an eternity. The "perfect" family, whom everyone thought we were, quickly began to unravel at the seams.

My stepdad decided that he would move to Seattle, Washington, where some of his friends and a brother had moved a few years earlier. He moved fairly quickly as to save face or what face any of us had left at this point. By this time, there were all different takes of the happenings going around. It never ceases to amaze me how such things spread like wildfire. It's unfortunate that such is a typical response instead of a fortress of strength and support being built among family and friends.

This was definitely not something I dreamed would transpire in my senior year of high school. What would all my friends think? Would they look at me differently? Lots of questions and concerns began to race through my mind. I remember my guidance counselor taking me for a walk on the playground at school. She began to weep and apologize for not recognizing the signs of abuse. I was quick to reassure her that the signs were really not apparent. I had learned to deal with the pain of what was going on at home by making others happy. It seemed to validate me and outweigh the abuse.

My counselor wasn't the only one who wanted to talk me. It wasn't too long before Child Protective Services (CPS) visited and then required that I go through professional counseling. So my mom made me an appointment, and to counseling we went. I remember my one and only visit with a man named Sandy, the counselor. We talked, and I explained what had happened and how I was able to deal. I shared with him that God was the only reason I was able to make it thus far without any noticeable signs of abuse. I explained how that God Himself had become my DADDY. How that even though the abuse was happening, I somehow knew that God was still taking care of me. That He was always there for me to talk to when I felt as though I couldn't talk to anyone else. The long and short of it was, Mr. Sandy told me that there was nothing he could say to me that would offer any assistance as I had my head on my shoulders better than he did. The truth is that it wasn't anything of my own doing, but God who made the difference.

At some point during the aftermath of my stepdad leaving, I was confronted about pressing charges against him. This seemed to be an overwhelming responsibility for a sixteen-soon-to-be-seventeen-year-old. I just couldn't bring myself to do it. I can't really give a valid reason why other than I was trying to protect my brother and leave what very little dignity our family had remaining. I'm not sure if anyone understood it, or even if *I* did at the time, but that was what I chose. Snarling remarks started from folks inquiring of why I would not do so. It was even indicated at one point that it would be my fault if another little girl became a victim of abuse. Trust me, I didn't need anyone to point that out to me. I only hoped that I had made the right decision.

The next few months were full of mixed emotions. Everything I had known was changing, and drastically so. My mom—a single mother again now with two kids, and teenagers at that—was overwhelmed, to say the least. How was she going to support us on her own? Reality was she had married as a young teenager herself, and that was all she knew. It must be instinct because she just did what she had to do but not without fear, remorse, hurt, and lots of tears.

I remember coming home from school often to find her crying. Honestly, it was hard for me to process as I thought she was not happy with the decision she had made of me. It got to the point that finally one day I just couldn't take her crying anymore. We had a little expression that we shared from time to time to lighten things up: "You can't be serious when you are naked." This phrase originated from a mishap we had a year or so earlier. For some reason, we were rushed for time, and she had come to take a shower, and I wasn't quite finished with mine yet. She was rushing me to get done. So as I stepped out, I noted that I was being watched through the crack of the door. I then tried to position myself so I couldn't be seen. In the process, I somehow delayed Mom getting into the shower, and she got frustrated and smacked me a couple of times to get out of the way. I later told her the reason as to why I was stalling, and she was devastated.

Shortly after, I heard the phrase "You can't be serious when you're naked" and shared it with her a day or so later to help ease her crushed feelings. So in my efforts to cheer her up, I stepped out on our front porch and began to act out the phrase. Trust me, within seconds, my mom begged me to come in as our neighbor was one of the deacons at our church. She promised she would quit crying. Yes, I came in before the statement became reality. However, anytime I would catch her crying, no matter where we were, I would begin to act like I was going to fulfill the phrase. She seemed to dry those tears pretty quickly. Silly, yes, but it was good medicine for her. Still to this day, we talk about that, and I sometimes even threaten to pull out the weapon.

As time went on, she became stronger and more confident that it was all going to be okay. We were going to make it. Not too long after we were adjusting to the changes, my brother began to really struggle with his dad being away. Truth was he always struggled with the lack of a relationship between them and yearned for one. He decided to go live with him.

This was yet more heartbreak for my mom. I started to feel regret as this seemed too much for my mom to bear. Part of me began to wonder if we'd have been better off if I could have just endured a little longer. After all, I would have been going to college soon enough and had a chance to get away from it all. I can now say that I know that no matter what the outcome of the truth is, the truth is always the best choice.

So yet again with lots of mixed emotions, Mom and I started the next season of life—back to her and me—kind of how it all began. She and I became really close during the final months of my senior year of high school. All we had was each other, and it took some adjusting, but that was what we did, and it drew us closer together.

With graduation approaching, we had lots of things to do to prepare. One of these was sending out graduation invitations. So we sent the invitations out to family and friends—well, to most of the family, that is. With much hesitation, I decided to send a graduation invitation to the address on the envelope of the letter my mom gave to me back when I was eleven. Remember, it was the letter from my biological father's mom stating that they had moved on with life and we should probably leave things as they were and not to complicate things. My intentions were definitely not to complicate things for anyone but rather to meet my paternal family. I prepared the invitation with a couple of my senior pictures enclosed but couldn't bring myself to mail it. All the what-ifs started to overwhelm my mind. I mean, what was the likelihood that they would even still be living at the same address? Finally, my best friend decided to assist me, and she mailed the invitation for me.

The waiting and not knowing was gnawing at me. Questions flooded my mind in the process. Did they get it? How would they respond? What if they didn't respond at all? How would I know? All those questions came to a screeching halt the day I checked the mail and there was a card from my grandparents, who still lived at the same address. I can't put into words the emotions I felt at that moment. Part of me was scared to death of what might be inside, and the other part of me was so anxious to see that I could barely get the envelope open. It was a typical graduation card, but more important was the handwritten note. It stated that my mamaw had talked with my father, and they would like to meet me.

Really? Could this be true? Finally, after seventeen years, was I actually going to meet my father? I didn't have to look at the names printed on guys' belts anymore. It was a dream come true. I mean, this really only happens on *Oprah*, right? No, it was happening to me. I was overwhelmed with excitement and fear all at the same time. Now what?

Well, the personal note also extended an invitation for me to visit them and they would fund the trip as a graduation gift to me. This was too much to process at once. They not only wanted to meet me but also wanted me to come visit, and soon. Their phone number was included in the note so that I could call and let them know. We could then start making the arrangements for a visit. Again, words to describe the emotions escaped me. All I knew was that there was a whirlwind of them and from both extremes.

After sharing the card with several friends and family, I finally worked up enough courage to call. What do you even say to your grandparents whom you have never met? I don't have a vivid memory of how that initial conversation transpired other than arrangements were made for me to visit. They purchased airline tickets, and then I just waited until it was time to fly out and meet them.

In the meantime, it was a bit difficult for my mom to process all that was happening. I think she had given up on the idea of this day ever coming based on the history of the situation. Now it was becoming quite the reality for the both of us. After all, it was just a visit, and I was practically grown, so not much would change. Well, we were wrong in thinking that as little did we know, everything changed as we knew it. Just when Mom and I thought things were settling into a routine, something of significance seemed to always make adjustments.

10

A New Beginning

Now was the planning for my visit to meet my newfound family. Again, emotions from one extreme to the other flooded over me. I was excited that a dream, a long-standing prayer had finally come true. On the other hand, I was extremely nervous as to what would come of our meeting one another. The situation alone yielded an indescribable awkwardness as I was basically going to meet strangers who were my immediate family.

So the day that summer—between high school and college—came, and it was time for me to board the plane to discover the other part of me. I did not anticipate how hard it would be to leave my mom standing in the airport as I embarked on this new part of life alone, at least without her as the mainstay she had always been. I had never been away from her like this, ever. Through the tears, I boarded the plane and sat anxiously, awaiting departure.

Wow, is this really happening? Is this really happening to me? This was something you would watch on TV or read in a book; it couldn't be my reality. On the contrary, it was happening, and to me. I was watching God's plan unfold right in front of my eyes. How amazing. Could it be that God did have a plan beyond the abuse I had suffered as a child? Could my life become something more? A resounding *yes* was His answer, and He knew it all along the way: "For I know the plans I have for you," declares the Lord…"plans to prosper you and not to harm you, plans to give you hope and a future" (Jer. 29:11, NIV). And wow, what a future—one beyond anything I could ever imagine.

I was ready for takeoff. My flight was to Chicago and then from there to Terre Haute, Indiana. Upon arrival at the O'Hare Airport in Chicago, it was announced that all flights had been canceled due to bad weather. Now what? I was seventeen and on my own, with no idea about the process of flying and how to manage through delays or cancellations. I hurriedly called my mom with the news of the cancellation and inquired of what to do next. She was in a bit of a panic as her baby girl was in one of the largest airports by herself. Who would look after me to make sure I was taken care of and make it to my destination?

She instructed me to ask a gate attendant what to do. I asked and was told that all flights were currently canceled and all rooms in the airport hotels were currently booked. It was late in the evening, and I had no place to stay. Flights were not being rescheduled to depart anytime soon. Mom told me to find a security guard and stick close to them. As I looked around for someone, I quickly noted that there was somewhat of a language barrier between myself and most of those working at the airport as they spoke Spanish. This limited communication with a majority of folks whom I tried to ask questions. Finally, I was able to locate a janitor cleaning up one of the waiting areas. I sat down in that area and waited. I ended up waiting overnight and just catnapped there in that waiting area until the next morning.

Still with no clear direction on what to do or any instruction of rescheduled flights, I decided to inquire of the gate attendant on the next steps. She told me that I would be added to the list of those needing departing flights. It didn't seem very promising as I could only imagine how long that list was. I also wasn't sure how my family, who was to be meeting me at the Terre Haute International Airport, would know the details of all the changes. It's not like I had a cell phone then and could just call or text and let them know.

Feeling a bit overwhelmed and very uncertain, I just whispered a prayer to my DADDY. "Lord, please get me on the next flight out of here." Sure enough, within minutes, I heard them call my name over the intercom, and I quickly returned to the gate attendant and boarded the plane for Terre Haute, Indiana. Once again, all things were working out as someone was working behind the scenes. He always is, even when it appears He's vacated your life.

The plane ride from Chicago to Terre Haute was quite a bumpy and unnerving one. The plane was a much smaller one with propellers. I do not care much for the smaller propeller planes. Thank goodness the flight time to Terre Haute was short. As they started making the arrival and landing announcements over the intercom, my heart began to race and questions flooded my mind. Would they recognize me from the senior pictures I had sent in the graduation invitation? How would I know them as I had never even seen a picture of them? Would they like me? Many more questions continued to scramble through my head.

To help them identify who I was, I told them that I would be wearing an "I choose to be a Christian" shirt. As I got off the plane and walked into the airport, which was drastically smaller than the O'Hare Airport, it was quite apparent who was there for me. I saw huge smiles and an older gentleman with a camera who was clicking at the speed of lighting. My heart was pounding! Here it was, the moment I had been waiting years for: finally the moment of meeting the family I never knew.

There they were: Mamaw, Papaw, two little kids, and a young lady. The young lady standing there with them turned out to be their daughter, Jacki. The two little kids were Jacki's daughter, Morgan, and son, Samuele. The ironic thing about Jacki was that when I found out I was going to meet my family of which their last name was Simmons, a friend of mine who had gone to Jackson Bible College in Jackson, Mississippi, told me to ask about a girl named Jacki Simmons because she attended Bible school with him and I reminded him of her. Could it be her? I could hardly believe it. I asked Jacki if she went to Jackson Bible College, and she said yes. I asked if she knew a guy named Kenny Gregg, and she said yes. How does that happen? Someone I practically grew up with went to Bible school with my aunt whom I had no idea even existed. It just didn't seem possible!

Hugs and more hugs transpired as we stood there meeting each other for the first time. I remember Papaw still snapping pictures with one hand as he pulled me in for a hug with the other hand. He didn't want to miss a second. There was an amazing amount of emotion in those first few moments. My fear of rejection quickly faded, and I was overwhelmed by the feeling of love and acceptance. Papaw called me his little Johnette as my father's name is John. He couldn't quit smiling and taking pictures. After all the pictures were developed, I noted that he had started taking pictures as soon as the plane peeked through the clouds and became visible. They were as anxious as I was.

After things settled a little bit, we grabbed my luggage and headed to the car. Jacki had to go back to work. My grandparents, Jacki's children, and I loaded the car and headed to Marshall, Illinois, where they lived. Needless to say, things were a bit awkward and quiet on the way. I do remember Morgan, Jacki's little girl, just staring at me. I finally asked if she wanted to sit on my lap. She smiled real big and nodded her head yes. She was about two years old at the time and quite adorable. After she hopped up on my lap, she looked up at me with her big brown eyes and said, "When I was your age…"

My heart just melted. She was too cute. From then on, we were bonded. She practically never left my side. As for Samuele, he was a little taken with the "new" girl. He warmed up to me pretty quick and said he was going to marry me someday. He was five years old at the time. Those are just a few of our first moments shared.

We finally made it to my grandparents' house. We unpacked the car, and they showed me to the room I would be staying in during my visit. Still, things were a bit awkward as I was grown and meeting them all for the first time. It took a few hours and maybe even a day or so for any level of comfort to be reached. There were lots of questions and stories to be shared. All in all, it was good.

It then came time for me to meet my father. He drove in from Iowa, where he lived with his family. Once again, the feeling of being overwhelmed came over me. The fear of rejection still lingered a little. You would think that knowing that he was my father would eliminate those types of fears, yet it didn't. I guess it may have been the backdrop of him not pursuing the efforts of finding me or being a part of my childhood that promoted the feelings of unease.

Our initial meeting was great. One of the specific details that I remember was him repeatedly commenting on my hair. It was long and blond. He had blond hair as well. I actually have our initial meeting on video but only recall having watched it once to date. Not sure why other than not really being able to put my hands on the video as it is packed away somewhere among countless VHS tapes of recorded church services that my grandparents had. Again, there was the sharing of many stories in the following few days we spent together.

At some point during our days of sharing, the topic of my childhood was discussed, including a generalized version of the abuse of my stepdad. I don't remember all the details but do remember one statement that caused a bit of tension. The statement was "If we would have known, we would have come for you." My response, in thought, was that if I wasn't worth it just because I belonged to them, I sure didn't want them to do so just because they felt sorry for me. I did express to them that I didn't need pity for the misfortune of the abuse. They should have wanted me just because. Although it was a very touchy subject, we were able to move on and enjoy the sharing of other memories from one another.

The weekend was scheduled with the meeting of one of my father's three brothers, Steve. He lived in Spencer, Indiana, where he was the assistant pastor and music director at a local church. We met at Cracker Barrel and had lunch. The meeting was again a little awkward at first, especially considering I looked more like my uncle Steve than I did my father. I even caught Uncle Steve's wife, Cathy, off guard enough that she asked if he was sure that I didn't belong to him. The ironic thing about it is they had a daughter, and her name was Dawnitta. Not only that, we looked like sisters. We both had long blond hair of which we wore in a ponytail, and from the back, it was easy to mistake us one for the other.

There was a special service being held at the church Uncle Steve and his family attended that weekend, so we all attended together. Apparently I got my musical abilities, playing the drums, from my father's side of the family. Uncle Steve played the bass guitar and sang. His wife played the keys and sang. Their daughter, Dawnitta, sang as well. Her brother, Steven, played the drums. Furthermore, Papaw played the guitar and the organ and sang. Mamaw sang. Jacki played the keys and sang. Her husband, Gary, played the guitar and sang. The only one who wasn't musically inclined was my father. He couldn't really even clap on the beat.

During the service, Dawnitta sang a special with the choir. I was absolutely blown away by her talent. She has an incredible voice. It was an amazing experience to have with my newly discovered family. We were definitely connected musically. Honestly, I was a bit overwhelmed emotionally by it all. Most of the missing pieces of my past were finally coming together.

My father, Dad, had to return home to Iowa after the weekend. I specifically remember a special moment that Sunday before he had to leave as he sat at the end of the dinner table and I sat on his lap as we shared our last few moments together. Yes, I may have been a bit older to be sitting on his lap, but it was as if I was a little girl enjoying the security of being held by her father. Precious moments to be forever cherished.

Then the time came, and Dad was leaving. Parting wasn't easy, but I was still overwhelmed with gratitude for the time we were able to share and begin our relationship as father and daughter. Yes, it would be long distance with a phone call from time to time and maybe a visit every so often, but at least it was more than not knowing each other at all.

It seemed like my time there flew by, and it was almost time now for me to return home to prepare to go off to college. It just didn't seem like enough time for me or my family. We decided to see if we could extend my time there for at least another week. I asked my mom, and she approved. We then changed my return flight home for a week later. Still at that, two weeks didn't even scratch the surface of seventeen years lost.

11

An Anxious Return Home

My return home was quite emotional as one can imagine. I was torn between the feeling of wanting to be with my newfound family and returning home to life as I knew it. Yes, I would now be able to communicate and visit with my father, grandparents, and extended family, but it didn't seem to be enough with all the time that had been missed. However, with the backdrop of starting college within weeks, that seemed to be the only feasible option at the time.

My arrival back home was nice as I had missed my mother dearly. And of course, she was happy to have me home. A few days went by, and I still couldn't shake the feeling of wanting to be with my newfound family. However, the overarching thought of leaving my mom tended to temporarily tamper with the desire to discover more of this new world I'd experienced. She had always been with me, and I didn't want to leave her there without me. The pull of the what-ifs began to override those feelings and the consideration of an already planned future to go to college at Northwestern State University in Natchitoches, Louisiana, where I had a full-ride scholarship. It just didn't seem to be enough for me to stay. I needed more answers. Did God have something else in mind for me?

By all rights, all my peers and mentors told me I was crazy to leave my education behind as my scholarships did not transfer. "It takes a college education to make it these days," they said. And yes, it all made sense to me logically, but my heart was definitely overpowering my brain. All I could think of was all that was missed and all the unknowns of the future. It seemed a bit much to process in my seventeen-year-old mind. Distinctly I remember my mother having to process some life-altering experience when she was the same age.

The pressure of what to do weighed heavily on me. I didn't want to make the wrong decision as my future depended on it. One thing was for certain: I wanted to do whatever my DADDY had planned for me. I knew deep down that there was a greater purpose for all the things that had transpired in my life. Therefore, I prayed and asked for guidance. However, a little less trusting of my own abilities to manage through that, I fleeced the Lord as Gideon did in Judges 6:36–40 (NLT) shared in context below. Some may disagree, but it's what I had to do.

> Then Gideon said to God, "If you are truly going to use me to rescue Israel as you promised, prove

it to me in this way. I will put a wool fleece on the
threshing floor tonight. If the fleece is wet with dew
in the morning but the ground is dry, then I will
know that you are going to help me rescue Israel
as you promised." And that is just what happened.
When Gideon got up early the next morning, he
squeezed the fleece and wrung out a whole bowlful
of water. Then Gideon said to God, "Please don't be
angry with me, but let me make one more request.
Let me use the fleece for one more test. This time
let the fleece remain dry while the ground around it
is wet with dew." So that night God did as Gideon
asked. The fleece was dry in the morning, but the
ground was covered with dew.

My papaw drove a semi for the trucking company ABF
located in Terre Haute, Indiana. I do not recall ever seeing
an ABF truck before visiting my grandparents. So I told
God, my DADDY, that if I was to move to Marshall,
Illinois, with my grandparents to let me see an ABF truck
on my own territory. One's initial response may be that this
was a no-brainer as trucking companies travel all over the
States. But not so fast. Considering that we lived in a very
small town, we didn't see many semis let alone named ones.
Most of what we saw were logging trucks as we lived near a
paper mill, Boise Cascade. I kept my fleecing to myself and
went on about living life as usual.

One day, my best friend asked if I would ride into town with her to drop off some papers at a local government agency. I agreed, and off to town we went. When we pulled in the parking lot of the facility, I noted an ABF truck parked across the street in a semivacant shopping strip. I was amazed and scared all at the same time. I must have screamed a little as Brenda, my best friend, asked me what was wrong. I quickly replied that nothing was wrong but everything was right. I had direction. I knew what I was supposed to do. Now the hard part was going to be convincing everyone else it was the right thing.

The convincing didn't go too well. My best friend, who had sent the graduation invitation to the address from the letter my mom received when I was eight, was now regretting even sending it as we were going to be roommates at Northwestern State University; not to mention all my mentors at my high school were certain that I would go to college and be very successful as a teacher. I do believe my mom was the hardest to convince. Or at least, she was the hardest one for me to share what I felt I was supposed to do. I knew this meant I would leave and she would be alone, at least without either of her kids at home or within a short distance of her. I felt guilty as she was always there for me and now I was going to leave her. But I knew deep down inside that this was what I had to do. Sometimes doing the right thing requires great sacrifice. However, the reward of doing the right thing is always greater than the sacrifice.

Time seemed to rush by, and I had to change my after–high school plans. I canceled my enrollment at Northwestern State University. In doing so, I was reminded that my full-ride scholarship was not transferable—one of the sacrifices. I called my aunt Jacki to make arrangements for my return. It was agreed that they would come get me over Labor Day weekend. Now it was the waiting until September to make the move.

Trust me, there were many times in the waiting that I second-guessed my decision, especially with the comments from several people. In spite of that, there was always this still small voice reassuring me that this was the plan for me. It was definitely one of God's mysterious ways. It didn't seem to make practical sense in human reasoning. Hence, this was why God said in Isaiah 55:9 (KJV), "For as the heavens are higher than the earth, so are my ways higher than your ways, and my thoughts than your thoughts." He has a higher perspective and sees the span of our lives at the same time. We, on the other hand, only see the present.

12

---•၄၇၁•---

A Huge Step into the Unknown

It seemed like no time at all and it was September. My nerves really started to kick in as this was a huge move for me. Again, I had never really been away from my mom, and now I was going to be hundreds of miles away from her. The reality of leaving everything I had ever known started to settle in on me. Yes, I was moving to be with my family but a family whom I barely knew and of which I had no history. I was definitely taking a leap of faith and trusting that my DADDY had it all as part of His plan for me.

Jacki, her husband, and their kids spent the weekend with me and were able to meet several of my friends and family, including meeting my mom for the first time. This was unquestionably a bittersweet couple of days. I was able to share a part of me and my environment with part of my new family. Yet I was thinking all the while that I was getting ready to leave it all behind and step into the unknown.

Wow, I never imagined how hard it would be to leave. I felt like there was no possible way I could actually go through with it. Maybe I would just stay for a few more weeks and then return home to life as I knew it. Well, that's what I had convinced myself of so that I could manage the pain I felt inside. It was as though my heart was literally breaking into pieces. Once we arrived in Marshall, Illinois, I called my mom and told her I couldn't do it and that she would have to come get me. So the plan was for me to stay until Christmas and then she would come for me. This helped ease some of my anxiety, at least.

But missing my mom was extremely overwhelming at times. We would call each other every day. And as far as I can remember, we have not missed one time, even to this day! The call may only last for a minute as we ensure that each other is doing well, but it is still part of each and every day. My mom is one of my most valuable treasures. I cherish her and all that she instilled in me through her example of loving God and others, as these are the two most important things in life. She is a big part of the beautiful of my journey.

Time went on, and I began to make a life in Marshall with my paternal family. In October, I started working in the jewelry department at the local Walmart. I looked at some local colleges to attend and ended up registering to start classes in the spring semester at Lake Land College in Mattoon, Illinois. So by Christmas, as you might have guessed, I decided to go ahead and stay. I did go home to visit my mom, and leaving her was by no means any easier. Again, I experienced the feeling of not being able to be away from her. However, after a few days, the feeling didn't seem as intense. So I continued to pursue life right where I was, trusting that God had specifically designed it for me even before the foundations of the earth, as declared in Psalm 139:14–16 (NIV):

> I praise you because I am fearfully and wonderfully made; your works are wonderful, I know that full well. My frame was not hidden from you when I was made in the secret place, when I was woven together in the depths of the earth. Your eyes saw my unformed body; all the days ordained for me were written in your book before one of them came to be.

Spring semester came, and I was off to college. Jacki's husband worked in Charleston, which was about twenty miles from campus. I would ride with him most days and drop him off at work before going to class. Things seemed to be falling into place until the middle of January, when Papaw became very ill and was diagnosed with lung cancer. They immediately scheduled surgery for January 29 to remove the lower lobe of his right lung. Surgery was successful. However, recovery would take some time.

During the process, I decided that time was too precious, and we had already missed much of it. I withdrew from my classes after about six weeks. I continued to work part-time at the local Walmart. This provided more availability for me to be close if and when needed. Papaw seemed to make progress other than being winded, especially when preaching during services on Wednesdays and Sundays. That did not stop him from making the effort to carry out his duties as a pastor. In April, he returned to work at ABF as well. It seemed as though things were on the up and up and we were returning to some form of normalcy.

That didn't last long. In July, Papaw became extremely ill. It was discovered that the cancer they thought they had gotten had now spread. He began heavy chemo treatment. During the days surrounding each treatment, he would get sick and become too weak to do much of anything. This was so hard to watch as he was known as a go-getter. It got to the point that he wasn't able to preach anymore. He just didn't have the lung capacity to do so.

There is one memory that sticks out in my mind of Papaw during this time. He was down at the church one day, piddling as he often did, and I went down for something and was heading over to Jacki's house for a bit. I didn't think anything of it and left the driveway of the church, and as I pulled in at Jacki's, I noted him pulling in behind me. He was upset and stated, very sternly, that I shouldn't leave without telling him good-bye. At that moment, it seemed a little drastic, but soon, it made all the sense in the world. He knew his time was short, and he wanted every minute to count. After that, I made it a practice to tell him bye before leaving if he was anywhere close.

Around November, he was put back in the hospital with little to no hope of survival. The hospital staff even went as far as to call in family and friends. He managed to hang on, and on December 1, we brought him home to spend his last days there with family. This was his request. On December 16 at 7:36 a.m., Papaw passed away. He had slipped into a coma during the night, and I wasn't able to tell him good night before I had gone to bed. It is something I still regret. However, the nurse who had come to be with us told us the morning of his passing to go ahead and talk to him as he could still hear us. So we all began to express our love to him. I remember Jacki began to sing him the song "No One Can Touch You like Jesus Can," and it wasn't long after that he drew his last breath.

I was now convinced beyond the shadow of a doubt that my move was meant to be. God knew what limited time we had and made the provision for me to enjoy being with my papaw for more than just a visit or two had I stayed back home and started college. Papaw often told me that I was his jewel and that I made his stars come out at night. I will forever hold dear the few but precious memories I have of him.

Exactly ten years and three days after Papaw's passing, my mamaw passed away unexpectedly. This was a bit tougher due to the fact that we were not expecting it and I had spent ten years with her. I definitely had more memories shared with her than I did with Papaw, but that by no means made his any less valuable.

13

---·೧ೡ·---

Forgiveness,
the Key to Facing the Past

As it turned out, two years after I had moved to be with my paternal family, my mom took a job at the same state college for which I worked in Terre Haute, Indiana. It was yet another answered prayer as her being over eight hundred miles away never seemed to get easier. After almost ten years, she then moved back to Wabash, Indiana, where she and I started. It was about a three-hour drive, which made it easier to visit more often.

My visits to see Mom soon led to me seeing my stepdad as he had moved back to Peru, Indiana, where he grew up and met my mom. He would come to my mom's to occasionally visit my brother, who lived with my mom at the time. The first time seeing him, I was a little apprehensive as so much had transpired since he had left after all the abuse came to light. However, through the help and grace of God, I had forgiven him. Now this is where some people check out, but let me share what I have learned through my experience. See, forgiveness is key in the healing process. We often think in the natural that if we hold on to bitterness, resentment, and even hate for the abuser that it is justified and they are getting what they deserve. The truth of the matter is we are only hurting ourselves. I once heard it put like this: "Bitterness is like drinking poison and hoping that the other person dies." The only cure to that is forgiveness, and the only hope of such is Christ.

It was in a moment of great loss that I again experienced the freedom of forgiveness. In November 2007, I lost my granny. This was extremely tough for me as I have memories of her all the way back to my early childhood years. She and I were deeply connected. Remember, she took care of me right after I was born to help my mom so she could finish high school. It seems that the more time or memories you have with someone, the harder the loss is. Again, please don't misunderstand. I am not saying that one with fewer memories is loved less than one of many, but that there is just more there.

I remember at my granny's funeral feeling this overwhelming wish for my stepdad to be there. At the time, he was still living in Peru, Indiana, which was not far from where my granny resided, in Wabash, Indiana. As I stood close to the casket with a clear shot of the door and who entered, there he was. I really do not have an explanation of the emotion that followed, but I crumbled. Finally he made his way through the line, and the first words he said to me were "I'm sorry, sissy." See, that nickname was the closest, in the natural, I had ever come to being Daddy's little girl. And even at thirty-six years old, it still mattered. So through the eyes of forgiveness, I was able to recollect many of the good memories we had as a family.

I cannot stress how vital and necessary forgiveness is for the healing process. Ultimately it is a gift that we give ourselves. It provides personal freedom from a negative response of retaliation or a mind-set of hoping that one gets what they deserve according to our standard. It is a choice we must make, and we are more inclined to do so when we understand that we are, in fact, forgiven. Not only that but also that we will need to be forgiven yet again. It is a biblical principle that if we withhold forgiveness, it will be withheld from us. And the truth of the matter is there is not one of us who lives without needing forgiveness.

Now let me clarify that forgiveness is not forgetfulness. It doesn't mean that what has been done is necessarily forgotten. One must use wisdom in their interaction with the abuser. And there are cases where no interaction or communication is best. However, forgiveness allows your thoughts and heart toward that person to be for the good of their welfare. Not for the hopes of their destruction for what they have done or even the personal efforts to punish them. Again, that does not do anything more than delay our healing and ultimate victory.

What follows forgiveness looks different for each of us. By that, I mean that not always upon forgiving does the victim have a working relationship with the abuser. In some cases, maybe reconciliation can be made. For many, this may not be the case, and that is fine. Reconciliation is a process that focuses on restoring the broken relationship. Therefore, if reasonable, this cannot be done without the strength of Christ to embrace the process.

One of the biggest issues to overcome is broken trust. This is something that takes time and unfortunately affects almost all our relationships following one of broken trust. It seems to change our perception of others and even that of God. Often times we tend to see God and our relationship with Him through the lens of our experiences in our natural relationships. Due to the fact that our relationships with our fathers, or others, are jaded by various negatives, many of us struggle with a skewed perspective of God. If our earthly father abandoned us, we struggle with believing, let alone, trusting the truth that God will never leave us or forsake us. If our earthly father abused us, we have a hard time understanding that bad things happen to good people because life is hard, not God; He is good. If our earthly father spoke words that put us down and degraded our value and self-worth, we struggle to accept the truth that God is for us and finds us of utmost value and worth, so much so that He gave His life for us. And the list goes on and on. It is imperative that we look only to God's Word to see Him for Who He is. He can and must be trusted. Only as we learn to trust God are we able to allow Him to help us in trusting others, even at times those who have betrayed our trust.

14

⊸•ℭℭ℃•⊶

A Family of My Own

In 1996, I married my mom's best friend's stepson. We were boyfriend and girlfriend when we were teenagers. However, when I moved after graduating from high school, I thought that was the end of that relationship. Little did I know God had that all planned out as well.

Our first son was born in 1998. We named him Kajun. I actually came up with that name from a bumper sticker of a radio station KAJN back home in Louisiana. I figured that since I wouldn't be able to give him a life in Louisiana, I would at least give him a bit of my roots in his name. Oh, how we enjoyed this little man.

In 2001, we had our second son. When I was four months pregnant with him, I had some complications that required a sonogram, and it was determined that he had a cleft lip. This led to several other sonograms to try and determined the severity of the cleft. Results indicated that it was his lip and palate that were cleft. We immediately began to pray and ask God for a miracle. There were several occasions that I was told by several different people that God was going to answer our prayer and our son would be born and there would be a fine line to show God's handiwork. I trusted that this meant that Rylan would be born without the cleft. When he wasn't, I have to be honest, I felt as though my faith failed me.

I couldn't make sense of the why in the midst of the situation. I felt let down by my DADDY. I began to question what I did wrong. Obviously I had done or not done something since things didn't work out like I had been told or perceived that they would. That was how clouded my mind had become. The days to follow were full of a vast array of emotions. One minute I was upset, and another I was completely broken realizing that no matter the why, I could not make it without the WHO, my DADDY. I reflected on His faithfulness to me and knew deep down that His promises were true. He had proven that to me many times before. He proved faithful yet again, and through medical science, Rylan only has a fine line to show God's handiwork. The psalmist David says it so well in Psalm 71:5–8 (NLT):

> O Lord, you alone are my hope. I've trusted you, O Lord from childhood. Yes, you have been with me from birth; from my mother's womb you have cared for me. No wonder I am always praising you! My life is an example to many, because you have been my strength and protection. That is why I can never stop praising you; I declare your glory all day long.

I think sometimes we are tempted to think that if we suffered pain and hardship in the past we have somehow paid our dues and life should be carefree. However, as long as we are here on this journey of life, pain and suffering are inevitable. We are living in a fallen world and are affected by the state of that condition. The hope is that we were not made for here. This is just temporary, so we must not fix our eyes on the here and now but look toward our only hope, Jesus Christ. The verse in 2 Corinthians 4:16–18 (NIV) says it like this:

> Therefore we do not lose heart. Though outwardly we are wasting away, yet inwardly we are being renewed day by day. For our light and momentary troubles are achieving for us an eternal glory that far outweighs them all. So we fix our eyes not on what is seen, but on what is unseen. For what is seen is temporary, but what is unseen is eternal.

15

The Only True Happily Ever After

It has been my observation that most women love a good novel or movie with the story line of a damsel in distress being rescued by her hero. There is something about this that moves our emotions. We get all giddy inside. However, oftentimes I find myself at the end of the story, asking, "What happened next? I want to know, did they kiss? Did they get married?" Ultimately, I want to know if they lived happily ever after. There is something inside of us that longs for that happily ever after, especially in our own lives.

Didn't our little-girl hearts pound faster when the prince rode in on his noble steed? Even as adults, we feel that familiar fluttering in our chests when love is conveyed with a glance, a touch, or a tender word. We love the fairy tale. We want the happy ending. We long for the prince to wrap us in safety and envelop us in his strength and fierce love. After all, isn't that what happens in Hollywood?

The reality of this longing is that it will only be truly fulfilled in eternity. Things here on earth only serve to fill our lives but never actually fulfill us. Christ is the only One who can bring fulfillment in our lives. He is our only hope of a happily ever after. Paul enlightens us of this truth in 1 Corinthians 15:19–20 (KJV/NLV): "If in this life only we have hope in Chirst, then we are of all men most miserable. But it is true! Christ has been raised from the dead! He was the first One to be raised from the dead and all those who are in graves will follow. Now that Christ is risen we have eternal hope."

So no matter what hardships and pain we have faced or may face, we must be reminded that our hope is not in this life. This is only temporary. There is a better day ahead. Our future is bright and *eternal*. The verse in 1 Thessalonians 4:17–18 (NLT) puts it this way: "Then, together with them, we who are still alive and remain on the earth will be caught up in the clouds to meet the Lord in the air. Then we will be with the Lord forever. So encourage each other with these words." Also in Revelations 21:3–4 (NLT), we are assured that "he will wipe every tear from their eyes, and there will be no more death or sorrow or crying or pain. All these things will be gone forever."

This is our hope. It is our happily ever after.

16

The Beauty of the Journey

So as I look back over the years and all that life has dealt me, one thing is for certain: all I have to offer is brokenness. Yet the amazing thing is that it is the very thing that God works with best. He takes our brokenness and makes something beautiful of it, as we await our true *happily ever after*. It is like the breaking forth of the dawn after a dark night. It is new and refreshing. The key is for us to give ourselves to Him without reservation, trusting that He is ultimately in control and He is doing a new thing in each of us. Scripture says in Isaiah 43:18–19 (NIV), "Forget the former things; do not dwell on the past. See, I am doing a new thing!" He had each day mapped before the foundation of the world began. Your broken heart, dreams, and life do not come as a surprise to God. He's just waiting for you to relinquish your will in trying to put the pieces together and make sense of your life to Him. He will then do what only He can do. He'll give you beauty for the ashes that you give Him. He'll make a masterpiece of all the broken pieces that you give Him. Bottom line is He created you, so He knows exactly how you go together. Be encouraged, and trust God with your life. He can and will take it from broken to beautiful.

Scripture Quick Reference

Psalm 34:18 (NLT)

The LORD is close to the brokenhearted; he rescues those whose spirits are crushed.

Psalm 51:17 (NIV)

My sacrifice, O God, is a broken spirit; a broken and contrite heart you, God, will not despise.

Psalm 71:5–8 (NLT)

O Lord, you alone are my hope. I've trusted you, O Lord from childhood. Yes, you have been with me from birth; from my mother's womb you have cared for me. No wonder I am always praising you! My life is an example to many, because you have been my strength and protection. That is why I can never stop praising you; I declare your glory all day long.

Isaiah 43:19 (NIV)

Forget the former things; do not dwell on the past. See, I am doing a new thing!

Lamentations 3:22–23 (NIV)

Because of the LORD'S great love we are not consumed, for his compassions never fail. They are new every morning; great is your faithfulness.

Ezekiel 36:26 (NLT, ERV)

And I will give you a new heart, and I will put a new spirit in you. I will take out your stony, stubborn heart and give you a tender, responsive heart.
I will also put a new spirit in you to change your way of thinking. I will take out the heart of stone from your body and give you a tender, human heart.

Romans 4:17a (NLT)

This happened because Abraham believed in the God who brings the dead back to life and who creates new things out of nothing.

Romans 6:4 (ERV)

So when we were baptized, we were buried with Christ and took part in his death. And just as Christ was raised from death by the wonderful power of the Father, so we can now live a new life.

Romans 8:28 (NLT)

And we know that God causes everything to work together for the good of those who love God and are called according to his purpose for them.

2 Corinthians 4:16–18 (NIV)

Therefore we do not lose heart. Though outwardly we are wasting away, yet inwardly we are being renewed day by day. For our light and momentary troubles are achieving for us an eternal glory that far outweighs them all. So we fix our eyes not on what is seen, but on what is unseen. For what is seen is temporary, but what is unseen is eternal.

2 Corinthians 5:17 (NLT)

This means that anyone who belongs to Christ has become a new person. The old life is gone; a new life has begun!

Ephesians 4:31–32 (NLT)

Get rid of all bitterness, rage, anger, harsh words, and slander, as well as all types of evil behavior. Instead, be kind to each other, tenderhearted, forgiving one another, just as God through Christ has forgiven you.

Philippians 1:6 (NLT)

And I am certain that God, who began the good work within you, will continue his work until it is finally finished on the day when Christ Jesus returns.

Colossians 3:13 (NLT)

Make allowance for each other's faults, and forgive anyone who offends you. Remember, the Lord forgave you, so you must forgive others.

1 Thessalonians 4:17–18 (NLT)

Then, together with them, we who are still alive and remain on the earth will be caught up in the clouds to meet the Lord in the air. Then we will be with the Lord forever. So encourage each other with these words.

Revelation 21:1–7 (NLT)

Then I saw a new heaven and a new earth, for the old heaven and the old earth had disappeared. And the sea was also gone. And I saw the holy city, the new Jerusalem, coming down from God out of heaven like a bride beautifully dressed for her husband. I heard a loud shout from the throne, saying, "Look, God's home is now among his people! He will live with them, and they will be his people. God himself will be with them. He will wipe every tear from their eyes, and there will be no more death or sorrow or crying or pain. All these things are gone forever." And the one sitting on the throne said, "Look, I am making everything new!" And then he said to me, "Write this down, for what I tell you is trustworthy and true." And he also said, "It is finished! I am the Alpha and the Omega—the Beginning and the End. To all who are thirsty I will give freely from the springs of the water of life. All who are victorious will inherit all these blessings, and I will be their God, and they will be my children.